WOODS & WATER,
WOLVES & WOMEN

WOODS & WATER, WOLVES & WOMEN

CHRISTINE BUTTERWORTH-MCDERMOTT

STEPHEN F. AUSTIN STATE UNIVERSITY PRESS
2011

Stephen F. Austin State University Press
P.O. Box 13007, SFA Station
Nacogdoches, TX   75962-3007
sfapress@sfasu.edu

LIBRARY OF CONGRESS IN PUBLICATION DATA
Butterworth-McDermott, Christine
Woods & Water, Wolves & Women / Christine Butterworth McDermott

p. cm.
ISBN: 978-1-936205-64-6

1. Poetry. 2. American Poetry. 3. Fairy Tales. 4. Butterworth-McDermott, Christine.

ACKNOWLEDGEMENTS

I would like to express my gratitude to the following—the editors of SFASU Press for publishing this collection, Margaret Moan Rowe and William J. Palmer who encouraged my study of fairy tales; William J. Stuckey, Chuck Wachtel, Marianne Boruch, Michael S. Manley, Maija Kroeger, and Mark Staunton who taught me how to write; Kelly Link for giving the right words of encouragement at the right time; Stephen F. Austin State University's faculty and students for their support; Dylan Parkhurst for his hours of hands-on help, Heather Hilliard and M. Brett Gaffney for editing the collection; my good friends Alison Baker, Matt and Jenae Batt, Amy Collins, Caitlin Conway, Amanda Franks, Nicole Hall, Michael Jaynes, Michael J. Martin, Jade Ramsey, D. Matthew Ramsey, and John Urban for offering ideas and encouragement; my Butterworth and McDermott families; John, who suffered through constant commentary about fairies, elves, and the Brothers Grimm; and Audrey, who makes me want to read all the tales again.

Thank you also to the literary journals and venues who first published the following poems:

The Magazine of Speculative Poetry:	"Second Encounter With The Wolf"
	"Snow Speaks"
Cabinet des Fees:	"Hansel"
Tales of the Unanticipated:	"Flounder"

"Flounder," also appeared in *The Rhysling Anthology 2004* (Prime Books)

CONTENTS

I. WOODS

II. WATER

III. WOLVES

IV. WOMEN

For my brother, who helped me get through the forest
For my husband, who transformed me with a kiss
For my daughter, who made me believe in what I couldn't see

WOODS

WEARY TRAVELER

Here at this house,
you cannot come closer.
You cannot cross the threshold.
There is no room for you.
So, you wander through the forest
like Goodman Brown, hand and hand
with the dark self you do not want to face.
You look for men with staffs
that turn into snakes. You look
for ways to worship. You kneel
and pray and then kneel and curse.
You know it gets worse: this path
leads to where there is no faith.

But there are other prayers
and other stories. You do not
have to tell this one.
There are other paths.
Here, let me show you
how this one leads past the briars,
past the witch's gate, hesitate
in the meadow here and the dark self
may find his comfort and let you go deeper
into the woods alone
where there is a cottage
with open doors and windows,
where you will be admitted,
where you will be transformed.

SECOND ENCOUNTER WITH THE WOLF

I did not realize how large
and white your teeth were
until you stopped me that day,
a year from when we last spoke.

The wind came by and flicked
the hood of my red coat
up around my head, blocking
the sound of your deep voice.

Perhaps the color was invitation
to your appetite. Maybe your lips
were dry as my throat. Regardless,
your pink tongue escaped and ran

over your mouth. Outside, in
the snow, it was like the most obvious
axiom, easily read. I was surprised
how I'd missed the lesson before.

Like a thousand snowflakes, memories—
your sidelong glances in bars and other
places towards the waitresses and cashiers,
my roommate, then my sister that summer

by the lake—whirl. I find my hand knows
what to do before I do and brushes
the hood down. I stand bare-headed, brave
against you and the wooded landscape.

KISSING THE BEAST

During our first embrace
I felt how fast your heart
beat. *My beauty,* you whispered,
and I did not know who

you spoke to; myself or some
other self folding in upon yourself,
some secret self you were afraid
to show, since it hid the wound

that made you cower and hide
the light of your power under
that mass of hair and claw.
I wondered if you could go

no further, if you were anchored
there—so I dug in, fingernails
deep. Through your fur, I
could feel the smooth

skin of vulnerability. I heard
you pant with fear. I placed
my mouth on your flesh,
licking away all those hidden

tears—until you were bare
and able to hold my body
close, until you could bear
the luminous connection.

NABOKOV'S SLEEPING BEAUTY WAKES

At first, she does not know the young man,
bloody and beaten from cutting briars,
kisses her. Instead, startled by the hot, bright light
she opens her eyes to the disk of the sun.

What had she been doing last? Oh, yes—up
a staircase, an old woman spinning, a sharp prick
that made her blood rush, the strange pulse of some drug
that made her lips numb, the fact she could no longer feel
her limbs, the tiresome bed from which she
could not rise, nightmares made real. Voices,
heard dimly as if through cotton: *A fever? A trance?*
She must stay in bed. Don't let her go roaming
about at night. Sleepwalkers are dangerous to themselves.
We do not know how this curse works. Another boy died
on his way in. Thorn bushes higher than the wall.
Give her nothing but the finest brocade, gold for her pillow.

She moves—past him, her savior—to the window
and sees the butterfly on the glass opening and closing
its wings, brilliant, then faded, then brilliant
again. She places her hand gently on the pane
until the insect's body seems to rest on her thumb,
She can almost feel the soft brush of wing.

She presses her whole body onto the window, kisses
the glass like an insect herself. If anyone looked
up from outside, they would see her poised
there, framed by red curtains, her hair loose,
her mouth parting and closing and opening again.

SNOW SPEAKS

Let me tell you what I've learned. "You don't know
what you've got 'til it's gone" and all that crap
happens to be true, especially when you wind up
 the housemaid for seven tiny men
whose bathroom etiquette leaves much to be desired.

No, I'm not saying I'd want to go back to the castle.
Face down Step-Mommie Dearest? No way.
You're not paying attention. My mistake wasn't
that I was too sweet or too kind, or any of that.
I was too blind. You see, I should've seduced him.

I'm talking about Hugh, the woodsman. I see him
sometimes down at the baker's and he's pretty hunky
under all that plaid. What was I thinking? "Snow,
you'll have better luck in the forest." Yeah, right.
All I came across was seven weeble-wobbles.

Heard he's married now. A few little ones, too. Sucks,
doesn't it? Why don't things ever work out for me?
Oh, the guy who bought the coffin? He was nice and all,
but I mean, he *bought* me. It's hard to click with a guy
who's expecting something for his tidy sum.

Yeah, nice how the Royal Court worked that one out.
Sometimes, I wonder if I'd have been better off
if they'd never jostled that bit of apple out of my mouth.
If only I'd opened up my bodice that day in the woods;
could he have resisted *that?* What if I had only said…

Well, hell, you can't think about the past when you've
got seven dwarves to feed. Stir that stew on the stove,
will you? Hey, at least I've got a job and the Queen
is dead, or so I've heard. Not that I'm going back to check.
At least, the dwarves don't mind if I whistle while I work.

ALICE CONSOLES ANOTHER VISITOR UNDERGROUND

Tumbling over in the dark you may claim
was a soft fall down a well. "Kinda swell!"
Not for me. No, it was a bit like hell—
which smelled like the sides of a kitchen drain.

You say I shouldn't complain. We should make
the best of this small break, enjoy our stay.
Well, let's go ahead and see. Show the way.
Take a day to see if you find it great

down here with Twiddle-Dum and Twiddle-Dee,
if you enjoy chats with Queens who lob heads
for breakfast. Rabbits who quibble, while they
nibble lettuce greens, don't sit right with me,
but you may find them a pleasure. Instead
of wishing you were dead. Yes, *you* might say

it's nice that dodos dance and lizards prance.
"It's fun how it's curiouser by the hour!"
You might be fine to run round blind when our
day unfolds its every strange circumstance.

I find it exhausting. The Mad Hatter
is bossy and frankly a bit handsy
when crossing laps to pour some cold, old tea
My pinafore's been soiled from the splatter

of the March Hare's chatter. The happy dreams
I'd once foreseen have all been now corrected.
I've tried turning heels and making appeals,
even wishing in threes, all the extremes.
Yet, each plea for rescue's been rejected.
No one here is listening to how I feel.

Even now you, too, are running away:
> "Goodbye, Miss Alice, it has been a blast
> discussing Wonderland, but I must pass
> on Chesire wiles and flamingo croquet,
>
> I'm finding the mock turtle's gloomy tune
> hard to croon, and I hate pigs in pepper,
> whispering flowers I can't decipher—
> Wait, can't I find a way out of this room?"

See, I've been trying to tell you: we're trapped.
There is no going the way you came. Come,
don't cry or we'll be in a pool of tears.
See, there's no grand plan on this twisting map—
but a friend gave me this piece of mushroom.
He says it dulls desperation for years.

UNREST

find the spell
to set it right,
find the witch
to close my
eyes again
you dragged
me up
how can you
not understand
my anger
try to know
it was like being
inside a rose
there was no sense
of blankness,
just a velvet
smoothness
of petals on my skin
I was open,
wet with wonder
in the world
of dreams,
where lilacs fell
scent over sense
and I rested
on a bed
of them
on the ground
angels did not come
but I hovered
levitating, liminal,
in some suspended
heaven—never dark

never night—
until you came
and flicked
on that light

HANSEL

I wake longing for candy. The taste
of crusty sugar on my tongue seems,
for an instant, to be an easy pleasure, but
nothing's guiltless. I can tell no one,
not even my wife, why when she turns
on the light, I double-over, nauseous,
into the bucket beside the bed.
She wouldn't believe the truth if I told it:
no one ever said not to talk to strangers,
not to take offered chocolates from aging hands.
I had to learn the hard way.

Now, they say I should've known better.
After all, I was the older of the two.
I was supposed to be the smart one.
I should have seen the sharp, eager look
that woman gave as she invited us in,
her smile drenched with spittle.
But I "didn't see past the meringue,"
I'm "an easily duped fool."

Everyone knows, of course, Gretel's aim was sure.
She gets all the credit for shoving hard.
Even now, years later, she's making a success
of it. Book tours and motivational
speeches. It just teaches you—
those who do the saving reign
while the rest of us dream
of some midnight where

we feel like we're seven again
licking crumbs from fingers,
devouring peppermint unabashed, being lured in,

lured away from whatever kind of life
we might have had.
No one cares if we're always waking up
in darkness, craving something unspeakable,
craving the moment of freedom
before the flick of the switch, craving
confection pushed through a cage.

ROSE

Each month, I wait, dreading drops
of blood that seal this fate. The wheel
turns and always the cradle by the bed
remains empty. Prince Charming,
in this mourning, you cradle me
in arms scarred with pockmarks from where
thorns stabbed you on your way in.
Healed over, they remain testament
to that dark journey through woods. No
one said life was a bed of roses, even though
you found me asleep on mine in the tower.

In this war of my own, nothing accounts
for bleeding, some endless punishment
for stopping blood and breath with
a spindle's prick—that hundred years
of aborted life claims this payback.
Fairies curse but what is worse is this
day-by-day charting of progress never
made. I've been resurrected with
nothing to harvest, trapped forever in
the white clothes of a lost princess,
stained red, but never blooming.

SCARECROW

for J.

Dorothy's husband thought
when she gazed out the window
she was thinking of all the
places she'd rather be.

She was charmed by munchkins
or would rather watch Toto
roll around with Lion in the back
yard or hear how The Tin-Man
dropped his "r"s down at the Club.

What was he really? A bed of straw.
The dark hollows of his face did
not make him handsome. He
scared no one and could not

speak in poetry of his love
for the way her pigtails moved
like long dark ropes
when she bent over the sink

to wash the dishes. He could
not hum a tune that would get
him into the Lollipop Guild.
He never had been able to say

anything quite right. This,
he told her one night when
the moon was a fireball
in the sky above their house.

She shook her head at him
and kissed his mouth, and
pressed her body up against
him—she was warm

like home—only better—
and she said, "You are
positively brainless."
She walked into the house.

He watched her red shoes
click up the stairs and they echoed
her words like a beautiful song:
my love, my love, you're wrong.

THE REAL PRINCE

has twenty-twenty vision.
He's off the charts, his optometrist says,
covering first the left eye,

then the right.
Click—*Is it better here, or here?*—
but for him there is no better,

it is all crystal clear.
It's easy to see past the false bride
to the girl standing there with her geese

as if there were a sign advertising
her true identity. Finding the hidden
princess is the game he's good at. He sees

that the girl on the bed in her death-like sleep
is still breathing deep, is still alive despite
cobwebs in her hair; he sees beyond

the dirty coat of Thousandfurs, sees
the glow of her true self. He does not care
that girl there was once an ogress

or an ogre's wife
or a fish folded into a bathtub,
or a beam of light,

or a bird.
He sees all their beauty
alive in the crook of an arm

or a mass of rolling hair
that used to be filled with snakes
or the rather stumpy legs once fanned out

to a fish tail.
Perhaps his sisters raised him well,
making sure he ate all his carrots

at dinnertime, that he didn't read late
by candlelight, that he always wore shades
in the sun. Everyone knows he could

have had a more lucrative career—
been a home run hitter, a fighter pilot,
an expert marksman—but he's a bit blind

to those other options. He's an addicted
agent of metamorphosis,
rescuing damsel after damsel,

defeating each witch. He admits
nothing's better than being a mirror
to someone so she can finally see

herself with perfect sight,
to make her awake from endless night,
to make her really understand

that true vision goes deeper than she can possibly plan.

DEVOURED

In our cabin, I watch my mother
gnaw on cake, half the bottle
of red wine already gone.

I've listened to her howl
her tirades—*most men are wolves,*
beware of how they're always

preparing for a sweeter, younger
morsel than the one they have
now—again and again. Her eyes

glinting, she points her finger,
dagger-nailed at my red t-shirt
and sneers, curling her lip

to show her teeth. *Girls like you,*
she hisses, her hate like steam.
She warns me I better keep

my mouth shut, keep my legs
shut, keep the window locked,
stay, stay, stay on the path.

I'm staring at the door,
determined that at midnight,
I'll bore my way through it

and run barefoot over the wet
ground into the forest, pine
needles sticking to my soles.

I am fourteen, more than ready
to stray among the trees. When that boy
kisses me, under the moonlight,

I'll let him bend my body back,
I'll let him take me down, I will
let his tongue fill my ear, erasing

every warning, what big eyes,
what big hands, what big mouth,
all the better, too.

THE CORE OF THE APPLE
for A. K.

Witches—good and bad—are reincarnated,
cheating death like black cats, except
with more lives—because if you think of how

often we step into the lane forgetting to look,
pass below elm branches about to crack,
walk under the overhang before it falls,

swallow too much of the potion, take the path
home with the wolf who won't tell us his name,
slip, trip into the oven, it turns out all life

is peril; the visit to the hospital is the exception
not the rule that heightens gratitude.
Like Snow White, we open eyes wide,

embrace life's kiss after death's apple,
promising we'll live happily-ever-after *from now on*,
we'll be so much kinder to all the dwarves, not just

our favorites, we'll forgive the evil queen and the father
who left us there in the castle, we'll give up our crown
and kingdom to help the poor *from now on*.

But *from now on* leaves us frozen in the forest,
too petrified to move, burying ourselves alive
in a different glass coffin. Truth is we land

on our feet much more often than we fear.
So the apple should be the favorite of our fruit:
succulent, red, ready to be bitten.

WATER

FLOUNDER

There's always a downside to being enchanted.
Just as I sink back to float peacefully through ocean chambers,
eyes staring straight up at the sun, I hear the plaintive voice
of the fisherman:
> *Though I do not care for my wife's request,*
> *I've come to ask it nonetheless.*
And I'm back to the surface again, helping him catapult his wife from
pauper to Pope.

The fisherman's wife always wants more and more.
He hasn't realized yet, there is no escape.
Sometimes I wonder why he's so willing to relay her demands;
she treats him worse the more power she gains.
Why does he want her to sit on a golden throne in luxurious furs
while he hangs back, a bowing, simpering servant?
Why doesn't he despise himself
like a proper man? I could sympathize with him, then.
I could understand that kind of loathing.

No matter what you might imagine, transformation
doesn't dim recall.
Fish body, human brain.

I still remember my last day on land. The long flight
up a cobwebbed stair,
the twisting and turning of every step toward the tower.
How could I forget?

Well, what do you want?
She was perhaps the most beautiful woman I'd ever seen.
At least she took that form.
Just a little rest, I said, *a little peace.*
I knew my voice shook, but she was a sorceress, a powerful one.

Ah, don't bore me, she sighed, gazing at her fingernails.
Don't make me angry.
She crossed her long legs. I saw the flash of calf,
white skin above a laced boot.
I had forgotten what wanting a woman was all about.

Let's be very clear. All I wished was for my wife to stop yelling,
for the blows to the back of my head to cease.
I just wanted to sit quiet in my own house for a change.
Take me away from her, I begged, kissing the white flesh
above the dark leather.
Give her whatever she wants, but let me escape.
She kissed me then, of course,
as witchy types are wont to do, and smiled.
She put me in this finny trap.

Sometimes, in my dreams—yes, flounders dream,
at least the enchanted ones do—
I remember what it was like to be human. In the moment between sleep
and consciousness, I feel again my arms fuse
to fins, my legs blend to tail.
If flounders could scream, I would scream.
Instead, I swim back and forth, hoping for the waves
to part like a portal
to lead me back to my bed, my clean sheets, my slippers,
a glass of milk, the sweetness of grapes.
It never happens.

I know the story's end too well not to propel
the fisherman and his wife
back to their original hovel, back to their squalor, their poverty.
Although part of me shrinks from the abuse the man
will take in the future,
she must be reined in. For God's sake, this kind of woman
will stop at nothing.

I know her kind…

always calling from somewhere, always calling through someone,
always wanting what can never be.

In the early days of the transformation, I studied the sirens
who lured the sailors,
broke their backs against rocks
in shipwrecks, dropped the corpses to rot
in seaweed netting like decoration.
By the time my widow gazed over the side of her lover's boat
into the deep water, I was ready.
Come to me, I sang through the silver water, *come to me*
and you'll have more riches than you can imagine.
The seduction didn't take long.
She dove down and I circled her body with pleasure
as it drowned.

It was only then I heard the other woman's laugh
and the echo of my fatal request.
Even now, I remembers the lilting voice that went through
the waves as my wife's lungs filled.
The sorceress gave me the power to grant wishes
should the need arise. *A fitting legacy. There is, you see, no escape.*

This is true. Each evening, in the dim and dark water,
I swim in and out of my wife's bones,
with a new understanding of what we both missed.
Her eyeless skull hangs open in a perpetual, soundless scream.

Someday, I might have learned—
as the fisherman and his wife will learn—
to not want as much, to find a way around the constant pleading.

If I had more time, I would have learned.
If I had more time, I would have asked
for a second chance in a hovel.
I would have asked for, I would have had, one last
fleshy kiss from that horrible, shrieking mouth.
I would have stayed home.

THE FROG PRINCE ADDRESSES
FAITHFUL HEINRICH

Well, Heinrich, I managed to escape,
and at this fast pace we'll be out
of the country by morning. Even though

she broke the spell I could tell she really
wasn't my kind of girl. All that whining
and far less gratitude than I deserved

for the return of her precious ball of gold.
Someone should have told her not to roll
it so close to the water's edge. What a brat.

Really a selfish sort if you ask me. Even
disenchantment was out of spite, some silly
spat and splat, I'm a flat prince against a wall.

No mythic kisses from pretty lips.
Sure, you couldn't expect she'd love a frog—
but a little common courtesy wouldn't have hurt.

She treated me less than dirt and still had nerve
to call herself a princess, expecting that once righted,
I'd be that knight in shining armor declaring my *amour*.

I figure they'll send the dogs after us for my breaking
the princely code of happily-ever-after. But we have
the head start. Ha! And we're a good team.

There's no comparison, friend, for loyalty
when I think of it. I can almost hear the iron bands
you placed around your heart to keep your sorrow

contained, pain for my pain, cracking apart with joy.
Your service shall be repaid, love. The final boundary
crossed. If you open your waistcoat, my human

heart will at last rest steady against your breast
until we are out of the country, until we reach the edge
of the sea, until we lie together undisguised.

WHAT I WOULD'VE DONE
WITH THAT KNIFE IN MY HAND

If I had been the Little Mermaid, I
just might've stabbed you in the heart to be free.
What kind of fool is grateful to a guy
whose best gift is permitting her to sleep

on a velvet cushion outside his door?
She wasn't the brightest shell in the sea.
But you shouldn't have escaped the blame for
how you treated her, or been so happy

with your new wife as she dissolved to foam.
On some level, you *did* deserve to die,
for kissing that pink mouth magically sewn
shut, playing with deep gazes in her eyes.

I would've kept score of all your tiny slights;
I don't approve of her dumb sacrifice.

With each step like walking on sharpened glass,
I wouldn't try winning your pitiful
love, just for an immortal soul. If asked,
I'd say it's unclear if you were helpful

to her at all. Perhaps she annoyed you
with all that mooning around. Or perhaps
the other girl had sweeter lips, or new
skills I'm unaware of. If I'm a tad

cruel, it's because of the evidence here.
You could've had my skepticism crushed
if you searched for her when she disappeared.
But you didn't. If I'd been her, I'd much

rather have no soul then let you be saved,
cleared for smooth sailing on those sinless waves.

MELUSINE'S HAIR

He was undone by the lush cascade of curl. Perhaps she should have told him the truth but her fear was (truth be told) he would love her for her hair alone, so she held her secret close—and made him promise to let her keep one Saturday each month to herself, locked behind a bathroom door. He thought it little to ask until his friends started wondering where she went, what she did. His betrayal took an instant, in a space as tiny as a keyhole. He placed his eye against the lock and saw her step naked from the shower, towel around her head. Then, she bent and loosed it and he saw a great unfurling, the shimmering like scales, like a red fish darting in blue water. He was startled by the plethora of waves and drew back, wounded by the astounding beauty which she kept rolled away from him, pinned into place like a giant piece of bread. It was, he realized, a living coil, slithering across the alabaster of her back. The inanimate brush was allowed privileges he had never placed his hands on. He was blinded and his resentment was strawberry blonde. He felt now her beauty was a gift she had saved for herself, which he did not deserve. He retreated and did not say a word, but what was forbidden ate at him at night until there were arguments and he hurled hurtful accusations. When she left, she did not wear a scarf—her hair shone like the copper bottom of a frying pan. He watched from the bedroom window, as she dipped her beautiful head into the yellow taxi. He turned as the car made its way toward the highway, away from the need to undo locks.

SEAL'S SKIN

Husband, to take me from the sea,
you hid my old skin
                    (God knows where).
To prevent my return home, you
hid my seal self on some high shelf

and dazzled me instead
with man-made treasures,
silks, diamonds, silver
anything I might ask for
to prevent my falling
out of love.

          Still, I have not forgotten—
I remember what it is
          to swim,
to be carried by waves to the shore
          and back again,
to swim
          against the tide on my own,
to feel myself inside a home
          of blue-green,

an aquamarine dream
that makes my face wet
with tears when I wake
          in the morning
          in this small house.
                    What I am close to
forgetting is why we are what we
are, why we have been as we
have been.

Careful.
Love is not a fixture.
You must find this girl again, love
her between new and old skins
        —or all that will be left
is an empty nightgown,
dropped on the bedroom floor,

earrings curled beside the sink,
footsteps leading to the beach
        where in the moonlight
you might see one final
glimpse of my silver skin
against the waves
        before I go under,
        without a glance goodbye.

VOICE

I'm sick of the oceans of silence between us,
my sister.

I can't help but think you'd be better
sinking once again to the bottom
of the sea with me, with me, love,

you'd be free again, no longer confined
to that rocky shore, your bare feet so sore,
a nearly clementine color from the scores

of cuts upon that dry flesh. Come, come—
don't you think there's been time enough

for you to surmise the looks he makes
to that girl with the money—Oh, honey,
it's not you he's in love with.

Can't you imagine what it would be
to feel yourself again draped in water

like me: the tightness of waves around you.
Fish abound in this wide, wide world.
Sister, you know only obliteration can

come from this obsession. Is it worth
walking on knives? The pain of his watching

her lithe body, ignoring yours? It's no surprise,
she'll be his wife and you will only exist
as foam in his memory. Come, come to me,

swim again, laugh, be free. Restore the
empty shell, lose your humanity, grow back
your fins, sing. Sing for me again.

THE RIVER IS DEEP AND WIDE
for M. L. B.

The witch sizzled like stew behind us
as we filled our pockets with her jewels.
"We have to get out of these woods,"
you said. "No good lives here." We
hurried through the trees, branches
nicked our skin, scratched
our bare arms and feet. You said, "We
have to keep this pace until the river."

A duck was the boat across;
that's the way it works in enchanted woods.

You let me go first, dear brother. My face
buried in the white feathers, I prayed our
father was repentant, our stepmother dead.
I did not expect when I raised my head
to see you turn back the way we'd come,
as if salvation lay in the land of candy
houses and rigid cages. But you hesitated,
then came over the river. When you
set foot on the other side, I did not expect
your eyes to be wet with tears.

When you took my hand, I kissed it in gratitude.

HER MOUTH

I.

She was going to sing but froze, pitcher in hand.
She'd been about to water the roses, but you stopped
her cold. You stare at her mouth, her parted mouth,
her teeth hidden in the dark like stars. And you think,
if only—ah, just this: a simple kiss, lip to lip.
That alone wills old wounds to unground themselves
and curses be reversed. But you turn as quiet
as an aberration can and climb the highest turret
of this cruel enchanted castle. You think she cannot
help but see you as Beast, ugly as sin, with your hairy
chin and chest, no cozy cuddly feline pet, but some rough
monster instead, paws as big as giant mittens, wholly unfit
for love. She tries not to sneer. You try to be patient.
You are compelled by the thought, *It requires only*
this simple kiss, the press of her dress to my flesh.
You should tell her this, but you are mute. You curse
yourself: what a fool to reach out for the grace
of her forgiveness just because you would be illuminated
in a burst of light. You pace the corridors back and forth
in the night. She comes and puts her fair hand
on your arm and murmurs, "Be still, nothing
like sleep comes from trying too hard."

II.

You could not deny her anything (despite her mouth's
beauty as it formed the question). Her father, ill,
surely has more claim to her affection than you,
poor creature. She waves goodbye and is down the road
as fast as pale blue slippers can carry her. The week
stretches long and then, longer. You know those demon
sisters hold her back. Look in a looking glass,
and see your love bound by tears made by onions.
You call for her at night, across the moors, across the air.

You call in your dreams and wander the empty castle,
devoid of its beauty now that Beauty is gone and you,
untransformed, are alone, dreaming of her little red mouth,
and her teeth like pearls, dreaming of her green eyes
and her raven hair falling over you like dark curtains.
Dreaming. Dreaming in pain for lack of her. You have
curled yourself down into the dirt near the roses. You
have forgotten when you last ate, when you last drank.
One night you sank here to dream and did not get up.
While you dream, she comes to you and throws herself
upon you in her grief. You rise up, are borne into the air,
your fur is hotly seared off to expose the unprotected human flesh.
She could easily pierce it with her Beauty if she considered
it, but her tears wash you over and over and you think,
At last, this kiss, only this—and your resurrection begins.

WHAT RAPUNZEL SAID WHEN HE FINALLY FOUND HER

All of that happened long ago when we were children. My hair now shorn, no longer golden; the babies grown, moved away. I live alone in this cottage in this dark wood, but I'm free from towers of stone and witches. I've dismissed prohibitions on thoughts and body. So when you come now, broken and blind, feeling your way, palms open to touch my breasts, I can take you in without hesitation, without pain of judgment. In this arbitrary love-making between old lovers, I can heal you. You never were my Prince Charming, but you will do. Here, in the wilderness, that's all you can ask for: a few familiar tears to soothe your scars.

FROG KING

Your hands cool my flesh
at night—
you run them
over my feet
when they burn
from too much walking,
and soothe them
with tea tree oil.

It is something like floating—
lying on your cool green
sheets, lilypads of bedding.
Your fingers
are so wet
and slick on my skin,
it's a little like drowning
but I am not Ophelia.

I do not want you
to transform into
a mere mortal man
who buys a yardstick
to measure the wood
for a fence around
the house.

I want constant
submersion in this
pool of the new.
I do not want
to break the surface.
I do not want you
to grow usual,
become known.

WOLVES

THE PRINCE OF SHOES

I always look up to the ding, in case it's her
finally winding her way into the store. I always look up
when the bell chimes. In truth, it doesn't chime. It makes
a honking sound: *waaaahn-woo*. This repetitive
waaaahn-woowaaaahn-woowaaaahn-woo is the main reason
I want to quit my job, besides shodding well-worn
faux-aristo toes, which sends me silent-screaming home
each day at five forty-five. She, by the way,
is the too gorgeous (*must kiss*) girl that lives three blocks
from my apartment on the second floor of that brownstone
two-flat. She's a girl with hair like electric gold
spun from God's cotton candy machine. I imagine the glory
up there, churning out gossamer reams (*I dream, I dream*)

She's the kind of girl that might come into the store just because.

You can tell she heeds fashion by the weave of her fishnet
stockings, her high-heeled Mary-Janes, painfully patent,
shiny in the sun like melting lollipops (*what a wollop*).
Her skirts are always pleated. Once as she leaned over,
I caught a glimpse of white undergarments.
It was the flutter of a dove—and then it was gone.
It wasn't nasty, but pristine. It made me long for
a cause to approach her (*I'm a flawed poacher
of innocent things*).

Of course, it's always the ugly ones that come on my shift,
the ones that waddle, the ones looking for comfort—a *low*
heel—the ones whose skirts skirt the floor, picking up
the grime, bringing it in. The ones who want a sensible sandal
and pull out their platinum cards to buy it. Once you put
on enough shoes, you know nothing accounts for taste.

I dream that some time, perhaps at noon, she arrives,
outfitted in a coat the color of pumpkin (*my plumpkin*)
and steers past the forty-something odalisques, avoiding

their practical pairs of crewsocks, directing her beautiful
gams (*wham*) toward those few designer pumps we keep
on display. She asks me to help her. And I take her foot,
caress its sole, slide her gently into the sparkling masterpiece
(*please*)—silver satin, all that freshwater pearl beading.
She smiles at the perfect fit. *Woo-waaaahn-woo.*

IN THAT REGION ABOVE THE STAIRS

Breaking down the door after she melted,
we found something unexpected. We entered the room
well prepared, but saw only a neatly made bed,

all that you'd call ordinary—organized papers
on a dustless desk. Only her closet left us
to guess, only the closet took us aback.

Her wardrobe, of course, was basic black,
surely to show off the vibrant green of her features,
the rather keen angle of her nose. No, it was

the shoes, and the stockings we had to peruse twice.
Each pair of pumps, side by side, arranged
by color, a glowing tide of rainbow fabrics, all

the toes topped with bows or precious stones.
They made us stare at one another. Was there some
dreadful error? Was she a different kind of woman

than we supposed? Certainly one can never assume,
but she didn't seem the sort who would obsessively cavort
in silk hose, in patterns of polka dots, pink roses, swirls,

dalmation spots, and countless variations on the red
and white stripes her sister made famous dead.
The way they were arranged, fitted together like

sleeping kittens, on a little shelf behind the door
made us pause a little more and cluck our tongues
in sympathy until we remembered the flying monkeys

and how she made ours lives ones of constant fear
with her "I'll get you, my dears." No pretty accoutrements
could erase the evil looks that passed her face and sealed

our doom. Still they did make us wonder long enough
to ask what had slipped in her past to cause her fashion sense
to be so neat while her soul was so, well, *incomplete*.

KNOWLEDGE

Each time you see one
at the grocery line
in her short shorts
or at the bank
with all her black hair
flowing or the girl
at the one hour photo
processing place
with her bee stung lips
ripe for kissing, it starts:
you picture yourself
grown ugly, you can feel
your nose hook,
your back hunch,
your eyes grow bulbous
with all that jealousy.

It's not hard then
to look at that white arm
flung across the floor—
a flag of surrender
against the oak—
and not feel a little
sympathy for
the purveyor
of the apple. It's not
hard to imagine
the satisfaction of seeing
the sprawling figure,
the piece of poison,
caught between the lips,
half-covered by curls
as black as coffins.

It's hard not to feel
the Queen's laughter
was a little righteous
as she stared
at the fruit,
almost pulsating there,
defining the heart
of the matter.

LETTUCE

So she was banished, so she wandered in the desert.
I, of all people, know she brought it on herself.
From the very beginning, she was always crying out
for what *she* wanted, never thinking
of the consequences, what it meant for everyone else.
Radicchio, cavallo, boursette, watercress,
rapunzel. Yes, it was always that first—*rapunzel.*

The longing for it came up from the womb,
flew through my veins, blinding me for want
of crisp leaves, the slightly bitter taste
sliding across my tongue, gnashed beneath my teeth.
Rapunzel—morning, noon, night—an incessant whisper
pounding in my head. All the time. *Rapunzel.*

It was in such easy grasp, growing as it did
in rows and rows in the yard next door.
The old woman tended each head with delicate fingers,
singing children's songs to coax them to fullness.
Still, she never smiled at me, not at me,
even when I was showing and every stupid bitch
I passed was pleased to pat the rounded mound
which rose from my once smooth skin. Take it,
I wanted to cry. Take it and all its infernal begging.

In the end, my husband went and pilfered some of the greens.
I could've done it myself. I could've plundered
without remorse, stuffed fistfuls into my mouth
like a frenzied rodent. I wouldn't have cared.
When confronted, I would've happily made the bargain.
Take the child? For God's sake, yes!
I would have felt no regret

but Martin was always the weaker of us.
Afterwards, he lived with it as if it were a gaping wound
from which all life ebbed—until he went away,
to suck at it alone. People expected when I heard
that she abused her, locked her in the tower,
that I would double over with some sense of guilt,
but I understood that girl. I knew what made her tick.

The old woman was duped by mothering.
I could've warned her that despite everything,
despite the years of care, doting, fostering love,
despite gorgeous clothes, perfectly decorated rooms,
the brat would have her prince, would bed him
while the woman slept below, would sneak him
into her room and would turn to lying to feed her desire.
Because want is always foremost and is never fulfilled.
She was always like that, even in her nascent form—
always calling out for what *she* wanted, never
giving a damn what it cost *you*.

They talked of how horribly she cut her hair,
scissors barely missing her lovely throat. Ah,
if it had been me, I would have cut all the cords
and let her spiral her long, long way to death.

EARLY FROST

He's dead now, but dreams,
he's always a black silhouette
running against snow, levitating—
arms flailing back, a sprinter

crossing the finish line, an in-motion
Jesus, the wind as his cross.
If only he had not lost his footing
on mirrors, lines of white snow.

If only he'd seen how transparent
your offer to him was—
but how could he resist
Turkish Delight, distilled.

Your winter won him.
The smooth sheerness of your body
on his burning skin; the icy flesh
of your fingertips on his hot

temples must have been like salve.
Nothing is more comforting
than to be pressed upon bedsheets
until you expire like a flower, held

to your beauty forever, splayed
but perfectly open in your folly.
Nothing could compete with the spell
you handed out, flakes of fantasy,

drew him in, bound him to the cold
that made him sick. Witch, we could
not warm him once you were through.
In fairy tales, the child is rescued

but we watched helplessly
as he puzzled out his existence.
We watched helplessly while
he froze to death.

DEAD WIVES SONNET

Bluebeard, have you found another beauty
with whom you can spend your sequestered life?
Do her honeyed lips call for you truly?
Is she pretty enough to make your wife—
or, in sunlight, does she seem commonplace?
Worse, does her sweet face remind you of mine?
It can't be that with each smile I'm erased
from your memory. No, love, I'm inclined
to say you remember, but think that bar
you pressed firmly on former circumstance
is locked. Fool. When women open your heart's
chamber and see all that damaged romance,
your cruel beheading of girls in the dark,
they'll fly like Furies and tear you apart.

LET ME TOAST YOU, MY BRIDEGROOM

You think I was persuaded by your kiss
and that's what led to our quick betrothal.
You seem to think I'd been dreaming all this
time of weddings and wasn't curious
to know of those old romances that left
you cold. Off limits to your lover

you marked your past and home. Yet to be loved,
I needed more than a mere promise and kiss.
I found that your mysteriousness left
me at odds with your good betrothal.
Oh, dear, how could I not be curious,
since I hoped I wasn't dreaming all this?

But, dear, I now find I must've been dreaming this—
while searching the woods for my beloved's
secrets, I came across a curious
cottage. Above, trees arched in a dark kiss.
Would we live here after our betrothal?
The moment I entered I wished I left.

The reddest blood soaked the floors. I was left
praying that I had been dreaming all this.
(But, what a dream before our betrothal!)
Collapsing, I wondered, what beloved
evil lurked in my unknown lover's kiss?
Rising again, I grew more curious

even though I knew that a curious
cat often dies. Down the hall, one door left
open, begged me to enter with a kiss
of light. Oh, how I wish I dreamt all this!
Dismembered girls who thought they were loved
hung on the walls in some dark betrothal.

A crone came. "Is *this* the home of my betrothed?"
I asked. She wrinkled her face, a curious
look. "'Tis the den of murderers, you lovely
girl—and they've returned, you've no time left.
Hide!" We both crouched in the dark. And this
is where you're dreaming I was swayed by a kiss.

Betrothed monster, I saw the girl you left
for dead. Just a curious dream? Perhaps. But this
is her finger, Love, and the ring you kissed.

CHERRY

That day, the autumn wind whipped the leaves
to the forest floor. She must have strode, head
down, along the trail until she saw him, lurking
there between the thin birches, waiting to leap out
and pull her in. We imagine harsh calls from a murder
of crows flew above them. Later, we heard rumors
about her mother; she did not warn her daughter
to be careful, had not told her how men would watch
her swing her backpack back and forth, salivate
as it barely tickled the pale insides of her bare knees,
how she should cover her bright red hair so it would
not shine in the sunlight like the skin of forbidden
apples. If only the girl had remembered her grandmother's
warning and swung hard at his head, it could have
saved her—but she was only thirteen and had other
concerns. Certainly we were surprised to learn
of the bottle of vodka tucked inside her bag
and we were surprised to hear that she'd been planning
to meet a boy up there in the woods. We were surprised
but then sorry that it was Peter Hunter, who discovered
her sprawled there, throat sliced, blood unfurling along
the ground like a dark red cape flung around her neck.
He sat there moaning, his face buried against the strap
of her broken shoe until they pulled him away. We
discovered, years later, that every December, he would
go back and trace her body's outline in the fallen snow.

SNOW QUEEN

Sometimes it's just the heat
coming off a human's skin
which makes me want to suck
them dry like oranges, some
are sweet as tangerines. Seducing boys

is always easier—
they leave themselves
so open to beauty, my icy kind
in particular.   All it takes is just
a sliver of a silver kiss, sparkling

like a diamond on an innocent
mouth. They shiver with it,
then burn away like furnaces.
The saddest part is how the fire
never lasts; every heart goes dark

with the cold. I've learned not
to care, to leave them there
like porcelain shells, like empty
refrigerators after feeding. What
happens then? Maybe they remain

among the ice-cubes, puzzling out
the metaphysics of frost, wondering
which arctic realm I've glided to.
Maybe they wonder what forced
me to be so frozen. Maybe they

wonder if they'll ever be warm again.
Maybe all they see is the flurry
of snowflakes before, in numbness,
they close their eyes to the
whiteness of eternity.

EAST OF THE SUN, WEST OF THE MOON

We walk against the snow.
I am hiding my wince from you.
I am trying to remember you are not the boys who held me down,
you are not the mother who failed to warn of wolves,
you are not the father who wanted and took,
you are not those who stained my snow white flesh,
you are not my fang soaked ravager. You have not tasted my blood.
It is only your face that makes me pause: bear rat tufted horned
creature snake beast owl. You hoot, angry only at night,
but still your sounds fill the morsel of my heart with fear.
          And yet, when you take my hand, clutched into a fist,
and uncurl it with your claws, scraping gently at the dry skin
I let you put into the warm center of my palm,
your tender tongue.

COYOTE DATE

I've done this for a while—the woods, the basket.
Oh, I've paid dues with grandmothers, but its
always been worth the prize—that delicious,
delectable girl, coming into the house unaware
only to say in the throes of that wide white bed:
What big arms you have, what big eyes.
But it was dark and the hood covered her head
and the hood was red which made me punch drunk
with ideas of meat, juice running down my mouth.
I've learned that I'm easily distracted at night.
In the morning a good look reveals that I'd rather
chew off my arm and leave it here under the covers,
bleeding, than wait for her to wake and smile.
What big teeth she has, what big ears. I long for
the woodcutter's axe. Here I lie, amazed I've gone
down the wrong path. You'd think my instincts
would've been better after all those little girls.

R. STILTSKIN IN HIGH SCHOOL

Queenie shunned him in the halls
unless she needed a poster or placard
for some contest.
He was happy to serve.
As if by magic, he drew all her best
out on paper so everyone saw what sometimes existed—
he made our glimpse of her real. She always won.

But she did not know him.

Sometimes she called him Robert, or Richard,
which were not his name. Once, flushed
with victory, she took his hand and whispered—
Roger, Roger—twice—*thank you*, the *you* drawn out
as if it were a mew of a kitten.

You've never read a fairy tale if you do not know
how he stood frozen, how he felt
the softness of her palm on his arm,
how all the hairs of it stood up in attention,
how his throat constricted when she said,
I don't know what I would have done without you,
how his head felt like cotton when he smelled her
candy perfume, how his heart ripped in two
when she unfurled her hand and raised it up
in a little wave goodbye. Her fingers
as they bent, seemed to wink at him, like eyelashes.

Yes, every part of her was alive and seeing
his true self, if not his true name.
Ah, his Queen, Queenie,
her beauty made his pen loop de loop
with long and loose depictions of what was and could never be—
*missed kiss, could I if I tried, for a simple, shining
moment could it be*—but she only cared for a crown
and a big blond boy who smiled

at everyone and everything and never knew
what it was to sit in the back of the room
trying to draw himself up, out of oblivion.

ANTIDOTE

The witch's plan for the unwary
always works like this: ugly though she is,
she seduces with the perfect offer:
> *I'll be your mother,*
> *I'll teach you how to spin, try*
> *this kind of peppermint, wouldn't you*
> *love a bite of apple, my dear, never*
> *fear, you won't be transformed*
> *for long.*

She always forgets to add
that you're trapped until someone
promises true love, sees your true glow,
and she doesn't give a crap about those things.

But the witch does not plan
for you to see what you're capable of.
> You can shove her in the oven,
> banish her forever, throw her
> on thorns to watch her bleed,
> ignore her insatiable need and let
> yourself out of the tower.

She does not expect you to be clever.
She thinks you'll march relentlessly
to your fate at the end of the hall.

She does not expect you to cut your way
through the dark by your own light.
She does not expect you to be smart
enough to commit matricide,
to find the pleasure in watching her die.

A DIFFERENT GIRL

What did Wendy see in him—
that ragged elfish child?
When he came to my window,
twinkling with need,
I ran to the closet and hid.
I must have been twelve, on that strange cusp
of womanhood, but still I knew enough
about this kind of boy. I knew promises
of adventure can spell danger.

Through the door I could hear
him begging to be let in,
so he could touch me once,
begging me to join the flight
across the sky towards unknown stars,
towards glimpses of mermaids,
towards lonely little boys who needed care.
We need you, he whispered as he cast
a liquid green light through the crack
under the door. I was compelled

but not persuaded. I gritted my teeth.
I squeezed my eyes shut.
I envisioned black holes and sea snakes
that lashed blue water until it was whipped
to a turbulent gray. I envisioned boys
so greedy in their need of love they tore you apart.

I sat still in the dark until the fairy light dimmed.
I sat in the dark until morning.
I sat in the dark, caring only for myself.

WOMEN

UNFURLING

Try to lock the gates to make everyone stay
in the gardens you design.

It will work for a time.
                But the hunger for rapunzel
passes—only existing when we are pregnant
with longing—a temporary stage.

Its beautiful leaves wilt with summer,
subject to blight and white worms. Hot days
only make the sky clearer and the way
to the ocean an open path.

                Try to stop me up
inside a tower, create bricks and mortar
with your lies. I know there is no firmament;

these are only words.
                My hair grows longer
than you may think. It sometimes reaches the earth,
although I braid and bundle and hold it up when
you're in the room. It is a secret bounty I will not
let you see—a nest of living ringlets. I know it could
serve as rope or ladder, a way to escape, to climb
down rather than up. Once I'm on the ground,

you'll be surprised to find I've taken
your keys and given them to anyone who might
be in need.
                All that remains for you
is a lawn of rotting lettuce.

YOUR HOSTESS OF FINE LIVING,
BURNT TO A CRISP

There's no question we bear some of the blame,
nibbling as we did on the delicacies of her gingerbread
awning, our hands sticky with icing. Even when we
washed ourselves clean, we still smelled like cinnamon,
a dead giveaway in this part of the country. We were rife
with poverty, and ashamed of this, we caved in
to her invitation, And we believed her beliefs,
surrogate as she was. *All you need is to make the garden
perfect, Hansel. All you need, Gretel, is to polish the silver
with care.* We built her confectionery empire
with our own insistent need for home and hearth.
But here's the thing, she could've just let us have a share.
After thanksgiving, we would have ambled onward—
still bereft, still orphaned—into the wider woods.
But we would have done no more harm,
our stomachs aching less. Greed fashions itself
in mysterious ways. She invited us in, and for revenge,
played mother, holding us captive in her stainless steel
kitchen, boiling concoctions on the stove.
And smiling, she told us how truly unlovable we were.
Inadequate. Ugly and unsatisfying.
And we believed her.
So, is it any wonder we rebelled with glee—
and watched with hungry delight as she moved
away from our dangling cages, laughed at her trip
backward towards the yawning pit of heat,
her spiral into fire. How could there not be
a certain cerebral joy as we heaved the door shut
on the sounds of her sizzling away like bacon?
How could we not relish the singular hiss
of her demise? How could we not find pleasure
in that last fallen soufflé?

CINDERELLA'S CHEF

Everyone turned and followed him to the kitchen. The whole lot
of them squeezed through the doorway to see the feast, the bird
on plate, accessorized with tiny potatoes and julienned carrots,
in a white wine sauce. *Deliciously decorated duck,*
one feminine voice coos. The wife hears the cadence behind
the wall. She stands alone in the dining room under
the chandelier, poised to move forward, but hanging back,
as if the heels of her shoes were anchored in wood.
She feels like Cinderella mid-flight at midnight, waiting
for the moment when the surroundings start to disappear,
when she is left in rags, forced to listen to the *ooh-s* and *ah-s*
rising and falling against the tile floor, on the chrome sink,
beyond the arch of the doorway. She imagines how Bettina
is laughing there, tossing back her hair, tilting her head,
revealing her long neck, looking at him with longing.
Melissa, too, bends her body towards him, rather than
the man she brought to dinner.
                              The men—though charmed—
will never admit the lure of his competence,
the gentle superiority of his perfectly prepared food.
A friend once asked how she could stand the way everyone
gawked, the way everyone seemed to be whispering sweet
everythings into his ear. *Can you show me how to make
that sauce sometime?* She knows she cannot be afraid.
Outside the kitchen, she knows how dim these voices
really are. They float into air and do not haunt the house
when they go. In the candlelight, her dress shines silver,
her hair gleams and the curve of her wrist is alabaster, her skin
far smoother than any of her guests. She knows these shoes,
stuck in wood, will be discarded. She will be rescued even
when they no longer fit. She knows that midnight here
never ends. The way he always offers her the first bite proves this.

AT THE WEDDING FEAST, SNOW WHITE RECOGNIZED HER RIGHT AWAY

I have no sympathy anymore.

    Once, I understood how you could
    look at me, and want to pull my raven hair out
    root by root. Certainly, it's hard
    when every day a mirror tells you what to do—
    feeds your paranoia by showing every
    chin hair sprouting out of turn,
    or the crooked leaning of the tooth,
    how the sockets hollow, how the skin
    grows thin and grey under eyes once round.
    Your leaching out must have terrified you,
    due to the world's love of circle and curve—
    the abundance of flesh and cheek and rosebud
    lips all around you. I could concur—
    it could make you mad. *Mirror, mirror,*
    on the wall a constant call in the head
    and heart, breaking you apart. Poor you

    until you turned inner hatred outward
    and offered up poison, comb and stay,
    and of course, the rich taste of tainted
    apple. Three times, and I rose again.
    I'm sure you suffered at my triumph.
    I'm sure you suffer at my happiness,
    my white dress, and crown. But I'd like
    to say, coming back down into the fourth life,
    I really have no time to waste, and do not care
    about all the things you may have suffered
    at the hands of fathers and husbands, villains
    and suitors, those who obeyed or betrayed.
    It doesn't matter. My only desire is to have
    shoes hot as fire placed on your feet, to make

you dance to your own extraordinary beat,
in tune to your own jealousy. You see
in the long run, I, despite you, have everything.

And you can eat your own heart out.

CONFESSION OF THE OGRE'S WIFE

They call him a cannibal. Their pictures
paint his face in shades of red, prejudice
foaming at the mouth, thirst for the tincture
of Englishman's blood dripping from his lips.

It's easy to vilify the dead. Jack
never gets his due, that thieving child. Good
sir, I ask: wouldn't you race to attack
the criminal who stole your livelihood,

your gold (the same hue as that bastard's hair!)
—and your pleasures? He didn't know the harp's
only magic was when my darling played.
Yes, wouldn't you run, blinded by anger,
pell-mell towards the fleeing boy's legs and arms,
not caring your steps might lead you astray?

And he, peace-loving sort that he was, would
come running after you, screaming your name,
"Ann, he's just a boy. It's not worth it, good
woman. It's only money!" But, insane

with your fury, you do not heed and keep
after that small thing—no bigger than what
those people call a rat. You, by a leap,
had nearly grabbed him, when your husband flew

up and pulled you back. "Think about karma,"
he said, and smiled. But still mad, you pushed him,
and that's when he tumbled over the side...
So, sir, I'd be grateful if you'd arm the
firing squad. Wouldn't it help put an end
to "fie fo fum" and all those other lies?

THE DIARY

You've heard about the others but only care
when he leaves in the morning, and you are left to wander
through the house.
                              What can you do
but wonder about hidden mementos of his past?
"I've just kept one gift from each of them, very small."
It's casual; in a filmscript, they'd call this line
a throw-away. Your mother says you shouldn't pry.
                              But it's like a sliver
of wood that splinters your faith, nestles in the skin
of your mind. It must come out.
A nurse told you once of a construction worker
who went into shock from that kind of festering
and woke paralyzed. You need to know what lies
behind that seventh drawer in his desk. A packet
of letters, a book inscribed, *Dear, dear?*
You, too, can be casual, surreptitiously opening
each closet, each cupboard.
                              You can call it cleaning.
You can hold the blue diary and say you are dusting.
Really, it is the door to all doors in your hand.
With one flick of your nail, you could open it, and have,
all the answers to what you are but are not.
                              You smooth the dark
cover with your palm, stroke the white sides, imagine the pages
are like ice cream and could be dipped into. You could lick
your fingers for knowledge, which would taste like passion
fruit and would tell you *(oh, it must tell you)* you are
the only one.
                              But, no, you (good girl)
set it down.
And then, there—the tiniest spot of blood red, just below
the binding. You dab with a tissue, hope for absorption,
holding the tip to the corner of that crimson drop.

But it gets brighter
and bigger, drying into the size of a dime, payback
for breaking and entering. Flushing, you relock the desk
drawer, turn off the light, close the door, grope through
the hall in mourning, thwarted by the agency
of your own undoing.

ON THE MATTRESS

Seven years into their marriage, she found
a golden stud under the silk covers.
How it had gotten there she turned over;
it made her wonder if the prince she'd known

had had some accident—perhaps a fall
from a horse, a blow to the head one day
while hunting. For surely no one could play
at being so stupid to not recall

their shared history, or his mother's test
with the same sized pea which proved her royal
sensitivity. Really, his loyal
vow should've stuck. She shouldn't have to guess

whose fair locks wound around the earring's back—
or what it was that a princess could lack.

PICTURE THIS

An incandescent flower of a girl,
luminously putting a tiny foot
encased in glass on the palace stairs. In
order to keep the myth alive, others
were given hideous markings on their
faces—that nose a hook, her one slanted eye's

higher than the other. So ugly, eyes
must be averted. Both innocent girls
shrunken, deformed, twisted, and maimed. All their
chances made improbable so one foot
can fit, so one can rise above the others.
These sisters silently keep it all in:

knowledge, the steaming envy that lurks in
their hearts. No one would believe that their eyes
darted over the heads of waltzing others
and knew in an instant who the blushing girl
in her mother's dress was—or that where her foot
had tread was obvious. Everyone there

was dazzled by her arrival and their
sour grapes would merely ruin wine brought in
from Rome. It's just a ball after all. A foot
over, some count giving Bertha the eye
was of more interest to the blonde girl
than the Prince, who she found dull. Still, others

like there to be jealousy and other
faults—abuse, hard luck. But she was just their
stepsister. She had the same tasks each girl
had in that household. Paid writers work in
drama to make things lively. They've an eye
for that. They set all sorts of things afoot

for a buck. Though funny how the prince's foot
fetish was never mentioned, or that other
than exceptionally beautiful eyes,
Cinderella was actually plain, or how there
were several whispers confirming, all in
all, Ludmilla was the most intriguing girl

of the bunch. It's just when a foot fits their
shoe, it's hard to allow other views in,
especially when the seeing eye is a girl's.

FAVORITE

She comes for Father when the cancer
has eaten him down to bone. She stays on the sofa
and I watch my boyfriend follow her around
as she strides room to room on long, tan legs.
Our little beauty always makes her mark.
Her dark lashes hit the bullseye of every weak man's heart.
It's been this way since she was fifteen.

I, on the other hand, am the sensible sister.

To be fair, she doesn't plan to outstay her welcome.
She's "in love" and shows me a picture
of a boy from school. I see nothing special: dreadlocks
and a nose ring. To each her own, I tell her.
In any case, she needs to hurry back. But I
beg her to stay. I do not need to rub onions
in my eyes; the tears are real. Living with her
perfection is worth some reprieve
from clinging tubes and catheters.

I walk in the woods while she sits in the room
and holds our father's hand. I wander among the trees,
reach out, touch orange leaves which crumble
in my fingers. I marvel at her goodness, her soft voice,
uncomplaining nature—and curse my own selfishness,
my own seeking of freedom from death.

A rose, the last of the season, blooms there
much worse for wear in the October wind.
I stroke its petals, tinged with brown decay.
I wonder if I pluck it whether it will
make me bleed or if, like everything else I own,
what flows within me has turned to stone.

When I return, he sits smiling at her,
as if solely her appearance offered healing grace.
His head bends to hers: a father and his only child.
It is enough
for me to wish I could run back
and throw myself on thorn bushes. No matter
how I fashion myself, no matter
how unrelenting my service, nothing
rescues me from the lack of Beauty.

DONKEYSKIN

Her beauty was the reason,
her father said. It was
his excuse
to come into her
room when the sun set.
Putting his hand over her mouth,
he taught her
how to hide light,
how to banish
the sun, moon, stars
under the soft bed of her heart.
The old woman
who helped her escape
said shine still existed
under tarnish, under cover,
but she did not believe.
She knew others
only saw the ratty
costume of her skin,
read the meaning of the dark
circles under her eyes,
She bit her fingernails
to stumps. She dressed
in shapeless sacks. She
hid everything she might
have been in dust.
It was only years later
when a brown-eyed boy
slipped her out of her old
wool coat one winter
evening and kissed
her bare shoulder,
catching his breath
at the glow of her flesh
that she started
to imagine life untainted.

And it was like a falling off—
a shedding of self—
she began to see
that beneath
the dirt covering her,
she preserved
the heart of a princess.

RESCUE

In dreams, I can't wake
I'm pursued
by old women who
hold sharp objects
on the stairs, and drive me
forward in terror

As in any good nightmare
I run higher and higher
til I'm locked in a tower
with no way out
but the drop down

My question for you is:
would you come through
thorns to save me
would you kiss the lips
of one who no longer breathes

would you resurrect me
no matter what it took
no matter who you slew
no matter what you hoped to find
would you come
through thorns

even if I wasn't the most
beautiful princess
in the world
even if I was just a girl
sleeping,
longing to be awake?

AT THE YEARLY SALES EVENT

It always happens like this. You start prepared:
heels, hose, nude bra. It's an adventure—who knows
what you'll find sifting through racks, hangers
clinking like money in a pocket as they're
flung back. Then she's there—*hag*—ruining
your day, stretching her arm over yours to grab
the dress you've reached for with her vulture claws.

Sigh. You went early to avoid such scavenging

You know what happens next; you're not surprised
when she pulls out that red sweater—as big as a potato
sack—with malice and says, "Here, Dearie, *this* will
fit you." It's just like the dream you had once where
you were Snow White and the witch was pulling on
the stays, hard—the yarn as red as that poisoned apple.

But you know better than to take the bait. You bite back.

You smile, you wait, you preen before the three-way mirror
in the dressing room. When she comes down that pink hall,
you pitch your beauty in her face. She must know seven
men or more would chase you. You are the fairest that
has ever been. No matter how she tries, she'll be left
to dance away, scalded by the heat of her own game.

IN KANSAS

Dorothy's changed since she's got back,
never doing her chores the way she ought,
always sassing me with this look
and rolling out these sighs as if it's all
so beneath her, as if she were Queen
and I'm just a servant she can't be bothered with.
Well, just 'cause I ain't never been to some fancy palace
with green walls or never had the luxury
of strolling—*la dee dah*—through poppy fields
with a talking scarecrow (if you ask me you
should be right scared to talk with things
not meant to talk) doesn't mean
I don't deserve a bit of respect.
After all, me and Henry took her in
when her pa split and my sister died
of a broken heart. But now the miss says
she knows something about that too.
Seems some tin man there—I swear I'd like
to say she was making all this up but
it don't seem so—this tin man needed a heart
and she helped get it for him.
Now she won't pump the well for water,
or dust, or peel the spuds. She just mopes
about talking 'bout how she wishes she had
them silver shoes, and could talk to people
who understood what she's gone through,
where she's been. And I say, "Why
dontcha just go back there, you silly child?"
"I would if I could, you old witch," she
says, "I would if I could." Since she's
got back, there's been nothing
but tornadoes in my heart.

WONDERLAND'S END

The pages of Lewis Carroll's diary for June 27, 28, and 29, 1863 were torn out.
As biographer Morton Cohen writes, "Something occurred during those three days that
caused a break in the relationship [with Lorina, Edith and Alice Liddell and their
parents]...No more visits follow, no outings, no photography, no croquet games, no
more walks together."

For years, the story has been that Charles was in love with Alice,
my sister; His heart broken by her burgeoning womanhood,
he pined for her child-self forever.
The story has been he was nothing more than a talented
pedophile, who never acted, but you can see by all those photographs
of half-clothed little girls, what he wanted to do.
The story has been...
Oh, my poor Dodo. No one sees you as I do.

The December night I last saw you, I wanted
to embrace your lanky body, beg you
to come back and finish the story.
What happened to that girl who went underground,
where did she go once she swam through
the Pool of Tears? I wanted to tell you how we—
the girls—were not poisoned against you,
even Alice, whom Mother warned daily:
You will never see him again. Stop asking.
I believed if I could just reach you, slip my hand
in yours, we could all fall into Wonderland again.

And then, as if by magic, beyond the green, yellow,
blue ballgowns milling about us, I saw you grin—
at me, at *me*, not Alice, not Edith,
but *this* Lorina. I moved toward your Chesire smile.
My mother caught my arm, held fast. I turned,
I twisted in her grasp in the aisle. When at last
I escaped, pushed through the crowd, you were
disappearing down a staircase. You hurried away

from the building, going farther and farther into the black hole of the night, to a place where I could never follow.

SILVER

My own mother, not some wicked witch,
told me how it would have been better
if I had been Rapunzel, born with long,
straight hair, grown to flow in sheets
to my ankles, as yellow as whipped butter.
And she pulled my head back,
shears glinting, and cut and cut,
until she made sure no one would comment
on my brunette beauty again: a beauty
so reminiscent of my weak father.
The curls fell to the floor like misplaced
commas until she swept them away.
Sentences remained unsaid, the clauses
all removed. We never spoke of it again,
but I learned my lesson: *Make sure to stay
clear of sharp objects*. I knew
the violence inherent in silver.

ADVICE FROM THE QUEEN

The women in fairy tales
are always mirrored:
girl and ghoul, one beautiful,
the other strewn with wrinkles,
maiden alone, then shriveled crone
doll and doppel, toil and trouble,
the gangly language of ever after
is always the same; there's only happiness
if you change your name,
become some docile princess,

and blame some other chick
for your plight. But blighted bitches
blast the pitch, forsake the riches
of matrimony (*phony!*)—and I'll tell you
it pays to be evil, it all boils down
to the taste of one good apple, one
satisfying crunch, one good lunch,
one nice deer heart for breakfast.

There's power in terror, being the bearer
of ill tidings, confiding bad news,
hiding under queen's silks—you choose.
You lose less as a harridan (*you can say
that again*) than being some prude afraid
to prick her finger, some teen twit
who's got a lot of living left to do,
and can't perceive how it's rather rude
to assume time stops when she's asleep.

It's only every now and then, when
the castle closes in, kept candles dim,
(*Jesus, how eerie*) and the moon's rim
goes shining in that damned glass
and you stand there freezing, looking
deep within the sweep of the reflection

that you might hear that idiot voice
(*why is it always after a long hard day?*)
say there's another slip of a girl
who's the fairest in the world.

After awhile the same old, same old
gets in the way of having a good day.
Still, I'd claim it's more of a thrill
having some clout, drifting about,
rather than staying so snow white
just in case some self-titled Mr. Right
thinks you need a kiss to feed
some deep desire you can't describe

if you tried, or picks up a vibe
that it only takes a simple fuck
to wake the supposed good girl up.
Hatred sometimes caters to freedom
(*that's my wisdom*). See yourself
in fair skin and you're closing in on doom.
Green potions and ominous portents
give you power, just choose the hour
you use them and do it carefully.

CPSIA information can be obtained at www.ICGtesting.com
Printed in the USA
LVOW061910261011

252260LV00002B/4/P

9 781936 205646